PARROTS

PARROTS

PETER MURRAY

THE CHILD'S WORLD

When you think about parrots, you might think of a brightly feathered bird sitting in a cage saying, "Polly want a cracker?" Most of the parrots we see in the United States are either pets that live in cages or birds on exhibit in zoos. In their natural jungle homes, parrots are wild animals that must find their own food, protect themselves from enemies, and raise their own young. There is a lot more to parrots than words and pretty feathers!

There are more than 300 different types of parrots. Most of them live in the warm jungles and forests of Africa, Asia, Australia, and South America. Parrots come in all different sizes. *Macaws*, the largest, can grow to be over three feet long! The small parrots we call *parakeets* are about the size of a sparrow. Parrots come in a rainbow of colors—green, gray, red, yellow, purple, blue—or any combination you can think of.

In the wild, parrots do not just sit around on branches mimicking human speech. Wild parrots fly through the forests in huge, noisy, colorful flocks, twisting and turning through the branches and landing when they find a tree loaded with tasty fruits or nuts. When wild parrots have something to say, they say it in shrieks, squawks, whistles, and hoots that only other parrots understand. Wild parrots are not interested in entertaining humans. They have more important business—they are busy being parrots!

Parrots spend most of their time in trees—eating, preening, climbing, and squawking at one another. Their feet are specially designed for climbing. Two toes point forward and two point backward, making it easy for the birds to hold on to small branches. Parrots can use their feet like hands to hold food, scratch themselves, or hang upside down from tree branches. Parrots are usually right- or left-footed—they always like to use the same foot for holding their food or scratching their heads.

Have you ever tried to crack a Brazil nut with a nutcracker? Then you know how tough they are. A large parrot can do it with its mouth! No other bird can match the power of the parrot's beak. Parrots' jaws are hinged at the top and the bottom, giving their strong beaks tremendous leverage. A large parrot can snap a broomstick as easily as you can break a pencil. No nut is too tough for a parrot to crack! The parrot's beak is not only powerful, it is also very sensitive. A special organ at the tip of the beak helps parrots pick the tiniest seed from its shell.

Parrots in captivity eat almost anything, from sunflower seeds to dog food. Wild parrots also like a wide variety of foods—berries, insects, nuts, worms, or anything else that looks interesting. Parrots love to play with their food! They like to hold it with their feet, look at it with both eyes, and feel it with their thick, pointed tongues. Parrots do not have a good sense of taste, but their tongues are very agile and their eyesight is sharp. The color, shape, and texture of their food is important to them.

Why are most parrots so brightly colored? You would think that their colors would make it hard for them to hide from their enemies! In the forests and jungles where parrots live, however, their colors work like camouflage. In a cage, a parrot might look like an explosion in a paint factory, but in the wild its bright colors blend in with the natural colors of the jungle. Even the brilliantly colored macaw is hard to see when it is perched in a tree laden with bright flowers and ripening fruit.

Some parrots can imitate human speech. One of the best talkers in the parrot family is the *African gray*. African grays can imitate human speech, the whistle of a passing train, or the meow of a cat. But do they really know what they are saying?

When you quack like a duck, do you know what the quack means? Just because you can talk like a duck doesn't mean you understand duck language! Parrots have the same problem. They might sound to us as though they're speaking our language, but they don't know what they're saying. This kind of talking is called *mimicry.* Do wild parrots talk? Only to each other.

When a male and a female parrot mate, they often stay together for life. Parrots do not build nests, as most other birds do. Instead, the female parrot finds a hole in a tree and lays three or four round, shiny white eggs inside. While the female is sitting on her eggs waiting for them to hatch, the male brings her food.

About three weeks after the eggs are laid, the baby parrots peck their way out of their shells. Baby parrots are just about the strangest-looking little things you can imagine! The squirming, pink babies emerge from their eggshells naked, blind, helpless, and hungry. Both parents feed the babies partially digested food. Within a few weeks, the babies open their eyes and sprout feathers. Soon, they look like small versions of their parents.

Parrots are always in danger from predators. Snakes, hawks, and wild cats will eat parrots if they can catch them. Parrots have powerful beaks, but they do not use them to defend themselves. Instead, they seek safety by traveling and feeding in large flocks. With so many sharp-eyed parrots keeping watch, it's hard for a predator to sneak up on them!

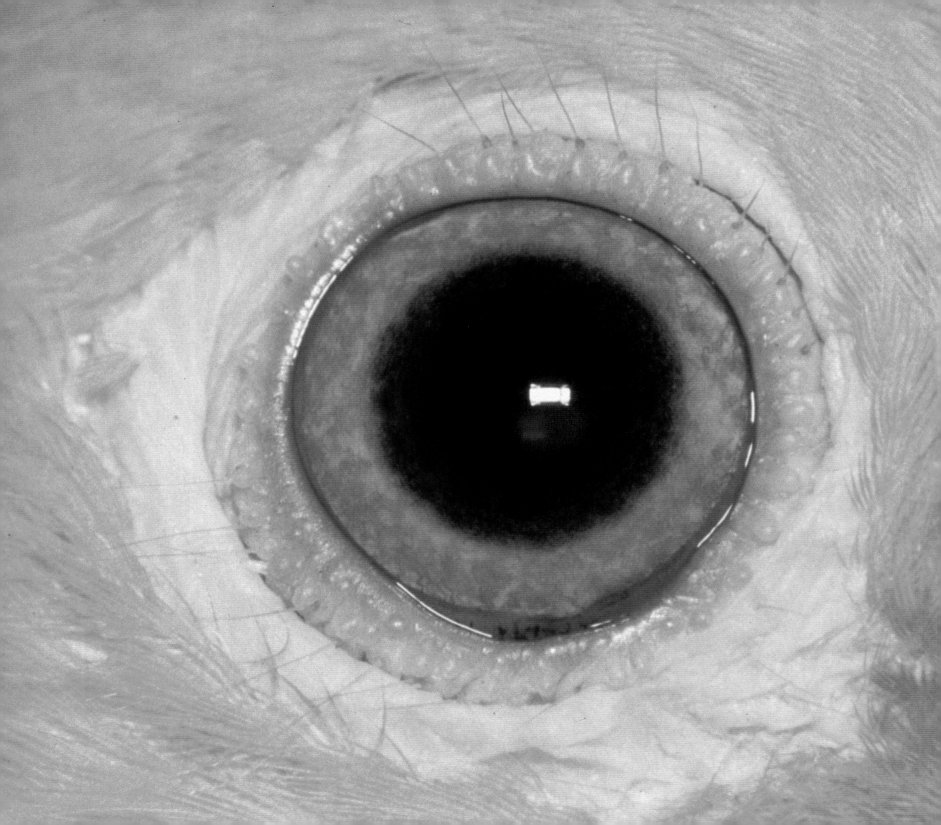

Less than a century ago, a parrot called the *Carolina parakeet* lived in the southeastern United States. Flocks containing up to 300 birds were common. Unfortunately, Carolina parakeets were killed by farmers who feared the birds would raid their fields, and by hunters who wanted their beautiful feathers. The birds' forest homes were cut down and replaced by farmland. By 1914, the last Carolina parakeet was dead. Now there are no native parrots living in the United States.

Wild parrots need places to live. They need plenty of fruits and nuts to eat, trees to nest in, and dense tropical foliage to conceal them from their enemies. If wild parrots are to survive, they need to be left alone. The rainforest habitat that parrots love is rapidly disappearing. Wild parrots are sometimes captured and sold as pets, or killed for their feathers. Many parrot species are now in danger of becoming extinct, like the Carolina parakeet.

What would the parrots say about that?

Awwwk?

INDEX

PHOTO RESEARCH
Charles Rotter / Archipelago Productions

PHOTO CREDITS
COMSTOCK / George Lepp: 7
E. R. Degginger: 22
Frank Todd: 11
Kevin Schafer: 8, 17, 27
Kevin Schafer & Martha Hill: 14
Robert & Linda Mitchell: 2, 13, 21, 28
Ron Kimball: cover, 4, 31
VIREO / S. Lousada: 24
Westlight Editorial Services / Bill Dow: 18

Library of Congress Cataloging-in-Publication Data
Murray, Peter, 1952 Sept. 29-
Parrots / by Peter Murray.
p. cm.
Summary: Describes the physical characteristics,
behavior, and life cycle of parrots.
ISBN 1-56766-015-0
1. Parrots--Juvenile literature. [1. Parrots.] I. Title.
QL696.P7M9 1993   92-44265
598'.71--dc20

Distributed to schools and libraries in the United States by
ENCYCLOPAEDIA BRITANNICA EDUCATIONAL CORP.
310 South Michigan Avenue
Chicago, Illinois 60604